Ice Cr
Kids and Cats

Written by Jill Eggleton
Illustrated by Trevor Pye

Rupert made ice cream.
He looked in his machine.

"Look at all this ice cream," he said.
"I will have a party."

3

Rupert made a sign.
He put it
on his shop.

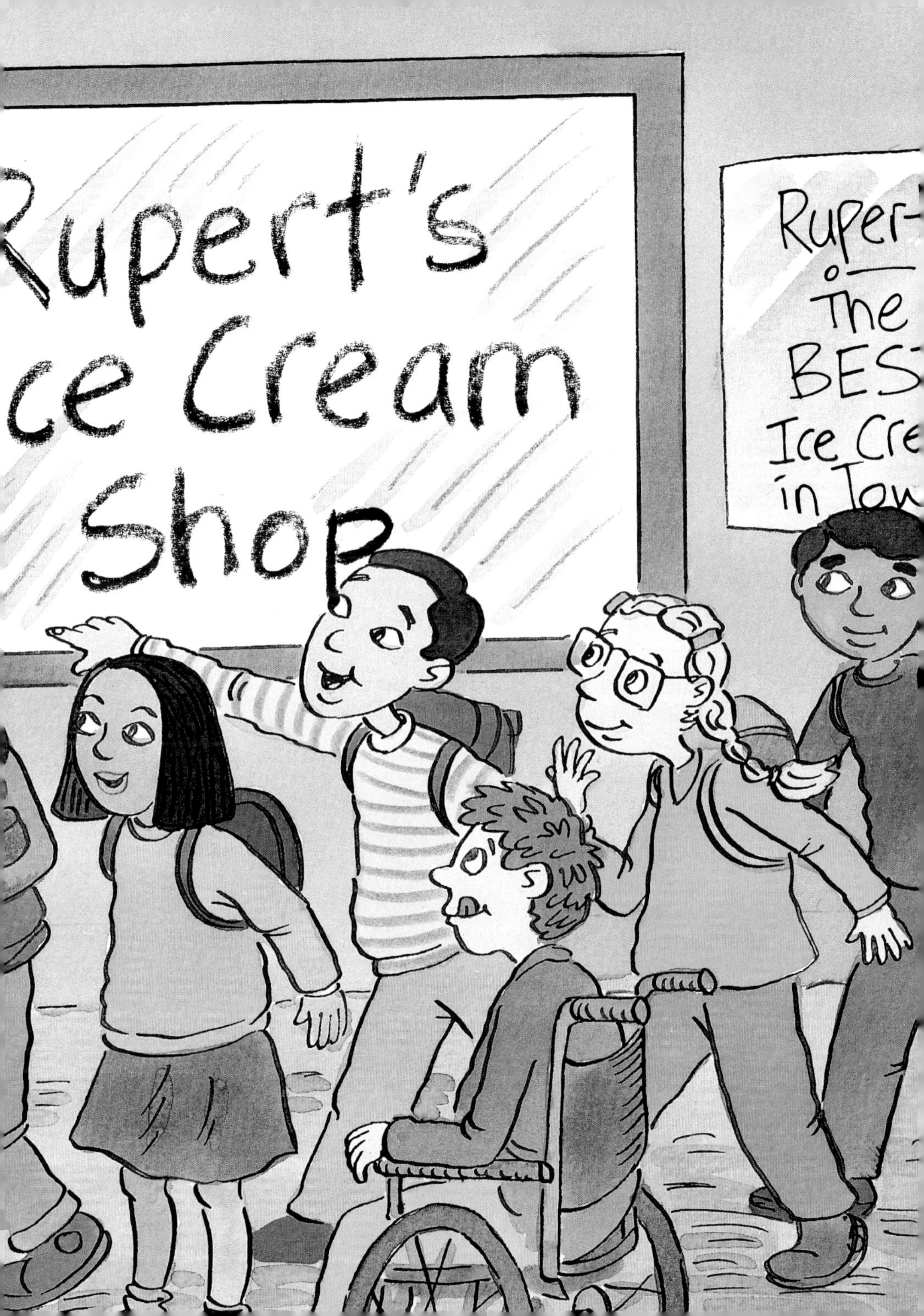
Rupert's
ce Cream
Shop
Ruper
The
BES
Ice Cre
in Tow

The kids came
to Rupert's shop.
But the cats came, too.

"No cats," said Rupert.
"This ice cream
is for kids."

7

The kids sat in the shop
with **big** ice creams.

8

The cats sat at the door
with **big** tongues.
Meow! Meow! Meow!

The ice-cream machine
went . . .
whirr, whirr, whirr . . . **Bang!**

10

The ice cream went
all over the floor!

The ice cream went
all over the shop.
"**Help!**" said Rupert.
"I have ice cream
in my shoes."

12

The cats went . . .
meow, meow, meow
at the door.

Rupert went to the door.
"OK, Cats," he said.
"This ice cream is for you!"

14

Signs

Come in for ice cream!

Free ice cream today!

Yummy ice cream!

Ice cream for cats!

Guide Notes

Title: Ice Cream for Kids and Cats

Stage: Early (2) – Yellow

Genre: Fiction

Approach: Guided Reading

Processes: Thinking Critically, Exploring Language, Processing Information

Written and Visual Focus: Signs

Word Count: 132

THINKING CRITICALLY

(sample questions)
- What do you think this story could be about?
- Focus on the title and discuss.
- Why do you think the cats came to Rupert's shop?
- Why do you think Rupert didn't want the cats to have any ice cream?
- What do you think might have made the machine go *bang*?
- What could Rupert have done with the ice cream on the floor besides giving it to the cats?

EXPLORING LANGUAGE

Terminology
Title, cover, illustrations, author, illustrator

Vocabulary
Interest words: meow, whirr, bang, machine, sign, tongues
High-frequency words: made, all, with
Positional words: in, on, over

Print Conventions
Capital letter for sentence beginnings and names (**R**upert), full stops, commas, quotation marks, exclamation marks